P9-ANY-682

LIVING IN A VIOLENT HOUSEHOLD

LAURA LA BELLA

ROSEN
PUBLISHING®

New York

Published in 2016 by The Rosen Publishing Group, Inc.
29 East 21st Street, New York, NY 10010

Copyright © 2016 by The Rosen Publishing Group, Inc.

First Edition

Library of Congress Cataloging-in-Publication Data

La Bella, Laura.
Living in a violent household/Laura La Bella.—First edition.
        pages cm.—(Confronting violence against women)
Includes bibliographical references and index.
ISBN 978-1-4994-6034-6 (library bound) — ISBN 978-1-4994-6035-3 (pbk.) —
ISBN 978-1-4994-6036-0 (6-pack)
1. Family violence—Juvenile literature. 2. Intimate partner violence—Juvenile
literature. 3. Spousal abuse—Juvenile literature. 4. Women—Violence
against—Juvenile literature. I. Title.
HV6626.L323 2016
362.82'92–dc23

                                                            2014049620

Manufactured in the United States of America

CONTENTS

INTRODUCTION

In February 2009, Grammy-winning singer Rihanna and her boy-friend, Chris Brown, a singer and actor, were driving home from a party the evening before the 51st Annual Grammy Awards. The couple began to argue, and as the situation escalated, Brown began to hit and bite Rihanna. He punched her repeatedly, choked her, and threatened to kill her. Rihanna's screams prompted neighbors in the residential neighborhood where they were driving to call the police. Brown was arrested, and Rihanna, who was nominated for several awards and scheduled to perform the following night at the awards show, was forced to cancel her appearance. Soon after the assault, photos of Rihanna's bloody and swollen face were posted online.

Brown pleaded guilty to felony assault and was sentenced to five years of probation and six months of community service. According to Jayson Rodriguez's article for MTV, Rihanna later told ABC's Diane Sawyer, in an interview for *20/20*, that she and Brown both grew up in violent households. Her father frequently beat her and her mother. She told Sawyer, "I said to myself, 'I'm never gonna date someone like my dad. Never.'" Rihanna reconciled with Brown after the assault, and Rihanna and Brown were photographed on vacation together in Miami one month later. The couple dated on and off for several years after the assault before Rihanna broke off their relationship for good.

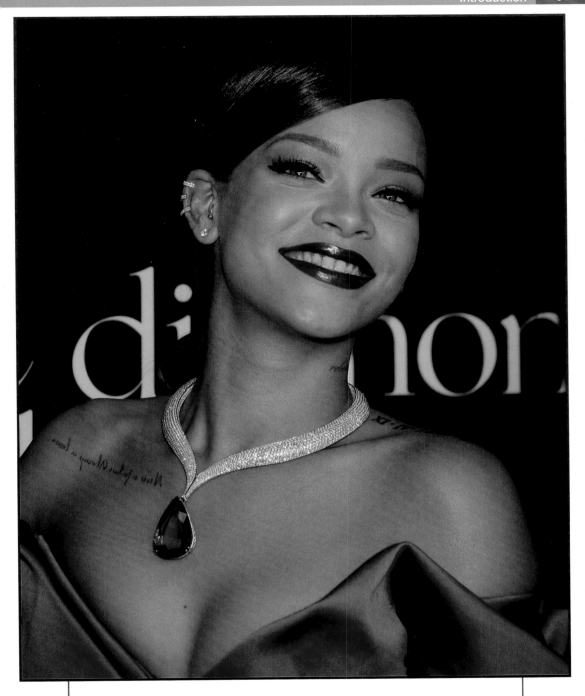

Rihanna, a Grammy-winning singer, was assaulted by her boyfriend Chris Brown, an actor and singer. Rihanna later said in
interviews that she grew up in a violent household.

The effects of living in a violent household can reverberate throughout your lifetime. Household violence, also referred to as domestic violence, can happen to anyone, regardless of age, gender, race, ethnicity, sexual orientation, or income. The effects and consequences of household violence are unsettling. According to Safe Horizon, a New York–based victims' services agency:

- One in four women will experience domestic violence during her lifetime.
- Every year, more than three million children witness domestic violence in their homes.
- Without counseling, girls who witness domestic violence are more vulnerable to abuse as teens and adults, while boys are more likely to abuse their future wives and children.
- Children exposed to domestic violence are more likely to have health problems. They become sick more often, complain of frequent headaches or stomachaches, and are often more tired and lethargic.

No one deserves to live in a violent household. If you find yourself living in a home where violence and abuse are occurring, you can break the cycle by getting help. There are many places to turn to for help for yourself and your family. Local law enforcement agencies can provide you with legal options, such as protective orders, that can keep abusers away from you and your family. In addition, local and national resources, such as domestic abuse hotlines and protective shelters, are available to help you, your family, or a friend find alternative ways of managing life in a violent home. By understanding domestic violence and its effect on your life and the lives of your family members, and by using professional guidance and advice from domestic violence organizations, you can get the help you need to escape a violent home life.

CHAPTER 1

What Is a Violent Household?

Hope Solo, the goalkeeper for the United States women's national soccer team and a two-time Olympic gold medalist, was accused of domestic violence in June 2014. The alleged incident began at a family gathering, when Solo's husband, former professional football player Jerramy Stevens, angered Solo by refusing to take her to the airport. Several friends and family members were

Olympic gold medalist Hope Solo and her husband, Jerramy Stevens, a former professional football player, have both been charged with assault after being involved in numerous domestic violence incidents.

present that evening. As Solo talked to her seventeen-year-old nephew, she grew hostile. According to police reports, Solo had been drinking. She charged at her nephew, tackled him, and called him names. The teenager suffered scratch marks to his arm and cuts to his ear. When the teenager's mother, Solo's half sister, intervened to protect her son, Solo reportedly attacked her, too. Solo pleaded not guilty to two gross misdemeanor charges of domestic violence. The charges against her were dismissed in January 2015.

This is not the first time Solo has been involved in a domestic violence altercation. One day before her wedding to Stevens in 2012, Stevens was arrested for fourth-degree domestic violence assault for an incident at Solo's home. According to police reports, Solo and Stevens had been drinking alcohol, and a fight broke out. Stevens was arrested but later released for lack of evidence. Solo and another woman each sustained minor injuries. In their report, the police noted that the victims were not cooperating with police.

Violence in the Home

Solo's alleged attack on her nephew and half sister is an example of household violence, which is sometimes called domestic violence. Household violence usually refers to violence or abuse that occurs between two or more people who are related, are involved in a relationship with one another and live together, or share a common living space, such as a house or apartment. This can include spouses, nonmarried couples, same-sex couples, family members, parents and children, or even roommates. Although domestic violence has often been used to describe violence and abuse in a household setting, the term "household or family violence" is now often used to recognize the impacts of violence on other members

SIGNS OF DOMESTIC VIOLENCE AND ABUSE

All people argue from time to time. Disagreements can be a healthy part of any relationship, whether it's between you and a parent, you and a sibling, or you and a friend. However, how you handle arguments can be an indication of an abusive relationship or violent household. Domestic violence can start with a parent breaking dishes, slamming doors, and screaming obscenities at you, your siblings, or another parent. And it can escalate to physical or sexual assault and verbal or psychological abuse. If you are unsure whether you live in a violent household, ask yourself these questions:

Does your parent or partner:

- Embarrass you in public with put-downs or demeaning comments?
- Look at you or act in threatening ways that scare you?
- Control what you do, whom you see, whom you talk to, or where you go?
- Keep you from seeing your friends or family members?

(continued on the next page)

According to the National Domestic Violence Hotline, on average, twenty-four Americans per minute (twelve million annually) are victims of rape, physical violence, or stalking by an intimate partner.

(*continued from the previous page*)

- Control your money by taking your paycheck away from you, making you ask for money, refusing to give you money, or telling you that he or she will get you what you need?
- Tell you that you're a bad parent, threaten to take away your children, or threaten to hurt your children?
- Tell you you're a bad child or threaten physical abuse for misbehaving?
- Threaten to commit suicide or threaten to kill you?
- Act like any abuse that occurs is your fault, or that your actions forced the abuse to happen?
- Deny abuse has occurred?
- Destroy your property or threaten to kill your pets?
- Intimidate or threaten you with weapons, such as guns, knives, baseball bats, or other items?
- Physically hurt you by shoving, slapping, pinching, choking, hitting, or pulling your hair?

If you answer yes to any of these questions, you may be living in a violent household.

of a family. Household violence refers to the harm caused when one family member tries to physically or psychologically dominate or control another family member.

The U.S. Department of Justice defines household violence as the physical, sexual, emotional, economic, or psychological actions, threats of actions, or threatening behaviors that are used to influence or control another person. According to the Office on Violence Against Women, these behaviors include any type of actions meant to "intimidate, manipulate, humiliate, isolate, frighten, terrorize, coerce, threaten, blame, hurt, injure, or wound someone." There are many different types of abuse, including the following:

- Physical abuse includes behaviors such as "hitting, slapping, shoving, grabbing, pinching, biting, hair pulling, etc." Physical abuse also includes keeping a family member or partner from obtaining proper or needed medical care or forcing the use of alcohol or drugs.
- Sexual abuse is any type of sexual interaction, attempted interaction, or coerced contact without the consent of the other

Domestic violence is about control and being dominated by your partner through physical abuse, threats of abuse, volatile behavior, and mental or psychological abuse.

person. This can include "rape, attacks on sexual parts of the body, forcing sex after physical violence has occurred, or treating one in a sexually demeaning manner." Rape can occur even if a couple is in a relationship or married.

• Emotional abuse occurs when one person intentionally undermines another person's sense of self-worth or demeans his or her self-esteem by using "constant criticism, diminishing one's abilities, name-calling, or damaging one's relationship" with other people.

• Economic abuse is much less recognized but equally as powerful as other types of abuse. Economic abuse is when an abuser attempts to make another person rely upon him or her financially. Abusers do this by controlling the financial resources of the other person, withholding financial support, damaging their partner's credit, preventing their partner from accessing money, or keeping their partner from attending school or from having or being able to keep a job.

• Psychological abuse is when an abuser uses intimidation to create an environment of fear; threatens physical harm to himself or herself, a partner, their children, or a partner's family or friends; destroys property; hurts family pets; or isolates the partner or their children from family and friends.

Sexual orientation doesn't make you immune to household violence. Lesbians, gays, bisexuals, or transgender individuals also suffer household abuse. In addition to the types of abuse outlined previously, lesbians, gays, bisexuals, and transgender individuals may also fear their partner outing them if they are not public about their sexual orientation. According to the Mayo Clinic, abuse in an LGBT relationship may include the following types of threats by an abuser:

- Threatens to reveal your sexual orientation or gender identity to friends and family, as well as coworkers or community members, without your permission.
- Tells you that lesbians, gays, bisexuals, or transgender people won't get help from law enforcement officials or that you don't have any rights because of your sexual orientation or gender identity.
- Tells you if you end the relationship or move out that you are admitting that LGBT relationships are wrong.
- Denies your sexual orientation or gender identity.

"Why Didn't You Just Leave?"

When people hear about women living in violent households or being abused by their partners, they often ask why they didn't just leave their husband or boyfriend and end the relationship. Unfortunately for women who are abused, or for children with no means of leaving, getting out and getting away from their abuser isn't always easy. Women stay in abusive relationships for a wide variety of reasons. Among the most common are the following:

- *Fear:* Abusers use fear to control their victims. Often times abusers will tell their victims that if they tell anyone about the abuse, they'll hurt or kill them, their children, or other family members. Many women stay in abusive relationships out of fear for what their abuser will do and to keep others from getting hurt.
- *Family:* For many mothers, staying in an abusive relationship is the only way they can keep their children safe when their partner is enraged. Some abusers will threaten a mother with taking her children away from her. To keep her children safe and to stay in the same house as her children, where she can monitor what

is happening, a woman may choose to stay with an abusive husband or partner.

• *Financial security:* To control their victims, many abusers will create financial dependency. Abusers will take their victim's earnings from a job, maintain only one bank account the victim cannot access, and provide a limited allowance to the victim. With no sense of financial freedom, many victims feel it is impossible to leave if they can't afford basic necessities such as food, clothing, and housing; can't afford to hire an attorney to begin divorce and child custody proceedings; or can't afford to

Leaving an abusive relationship is complicated, especially if children are involved or one partner controls the finances. Abusers also create an environment of dependency where victims feel they can't leave.

move away from their abuser and establish a new life.

• **Isolation:** Abusers seek to control everything about their victims' lives, from whom they talk to and see, to what they are allowed to wear, to where they can go. Many abusers isolate their victims to create a sense of dependency. They keep their victims from their families and friends, or they tell their victims that if they tell anyone about the abuse they will hurt the victims' loved ones. Victims often find themselves feeling like there is no one to turn to, nowhere safe to go, and no one who can help them.

• **Shame:** Being ashamed for allowing themselves to be manipulated and abused by their partner is powerful enough to keep women from leaving abusive partners. They feel shame for their decision to stay, and they feel they may bring shame and embarrassment to their family if people found out about the abuse.

• **Love:** Many victims, despite being mistreated in severe ways, feel deeply conflicting emotions toward their partners. They are in love with someone who hurts them. Many victims report that when their partner is not being abusive, they act like a normal couple. They go out to dinner, see friends, and travel. Many victims also say they believe their abusers when they say they will change, seek help through counseling, or stop the abuse.

MYTHS and *FACTS*

ABOUT LIVING IN A VIOLENT HOUSEHOLD

MYTH Domestic violence is an uncommon occurrence.

 One out of four women is affected by domestic violence. Although men can also be abused, women make up approximately 97 percent of domestic violence survivors. Household violence also happens as much in heterosexual as it does in homosexual relationships.

MYTH Middle-class women and white women are not as abused as often as poor or black women.

 Household violence happens no matter your income, race, ethnicity, education level, or sexual preference.

MYTH An abuser is not a loving partner or parent.

 Abusers do not constantly abuse their partners or children. Abusers can go through long periods of peacefulness and can be very loving and caring toward their partner and children.

CHAPTER 2

What Creates a Violent Household?

Jennifer Gardiner was divorced with two young children when she started dating her boyfriend. At first he hit her very infrequently, once every six months, and always after a major argument. In between he was loving and sweet to her and her kids. But as he began to abuse prescription drugs and alcohol, he grew more violent. Five years into the relationship Gardiner found out she was pregnant. She thought the abuse would end now that she was expecting a baby, but it only grew worse. When Gardiner went to the hospital to deliver her son, she had a black eye.

Soon after the baby was born, Gardiner's boyfriend began having schizophrenic episodes from mixing prescription drugs and alcohol. He also started having episodes of paranoia. One night, just before their son's first birthday, Gardiner and her boyfriend went out to a concert. The crowd and noise aggravated her boyfriend, so Gardiner took him home. In the car, she thought he was going to be sick and throw up. She pulled over and rolled down the passenger side window for him. She pushed him toward the opening to keep him from throwing up in the car. Drunk and high on drugs, her boyfriend thought Gardiner was trying to kill him by pushing him out of the car. He attacked Gardiner.

CULTURALLY ACCEPTED VIOLENCE

In some cultures, violence against women and children is culturally and socially acceptable. Culturally and socially normal behaviors are rules within a specific cultural or social group, often unspoken, that define how a community as a whole acts as well as what is accepted as normal behavior. According to "Violence Prevention, The Evidence: Changing Cultural and Social Norms that Support Violence," the World Health Organization's briefing on violence prevention around the world, the following are examples of violence against women that are culturally and socially accepted in some parts of the world:

- In India, Nigeria, and Ghana, a man has a right to assert power over a woman and is socially superior.
- In South Africa and China, physical violence is an acceptable way to resolve conflicts within a relationship.
- In Israel, a woman is responsible for making a marriage work.
- In Pakistan, sex is a man's right in a marriage.
- In South Africa, sexual violence is an acceptable way of putting women in their place or punishing them.
- In the United States, sexual violence, such as rape, is shameful for the victim, which prevents reporting of many sexually based crimes.
- In Jordan, a man's honor is linked to a woman's sexual behavior, and any sexual behavior deemed abnormal, including premarital sex or being raped, disgraces the entire family and can then lead to honor killings.
- In the United Kingdom, reporting youth violence or bullying is unacceptable.

Gardiner spent four days in the intensive care unit at the local hospital. Her boyfriend broke all of the bones in the left side of her face and her nose. She needed reconstructive surgery and continues to suffer from an assortment of medical issues resulting from the attack. She pressed charges, and her boyfriend was sent to prison for seven years.

The Need for Control

Domestic violence often starts when one partner feels the need to control and dominate the other. Abusers may feel a need to control their partners because they suffer from low self-esteem or extreme jealousy, they have difficulties in controlling or managing anger and other intense emotions, or they feel inferior to the other person in education and socioeconomic background. Some men with very traditional beliefs may think they have the right to control women and that women aren't equal to men.

A Learned Behavior

Abusers often learn violent behavior from their family, people in their community, and other cultural influences as they grow up. Some abusers have witnessed violence in their homes or may have been victims of domestic violence themselves. Often, children who witness household violence or are the victims of domestic violence learn to believe that violence is a normal, reasonable, or common way to resolve conflict, control behavior, or treat another person. Boys who learn from their fathers—or from other men in their family or community—that women are not to be valued, respected, or appreciated and who witness violence directed at girls and women are much more likely to abuse women when they reach adulthood.

Alcohol and drug abuse make domestic violence worse.
Substance abuse impairs control over emotions, and an abuser
who drinks or takes drugs is more likely to become violent.

Girls who witness domestic violence in their families or are victims of household violence are more likely to be abused by their boyfriends or husbands.

The influence of alcohol and drugs can contribute to violent behavior. A parent or partner who is drunk or high is less likely to maintain control of emotions and more likely to give in to violence impulses than someone who does not abuse alcohol or take drugs.

SIBLING ABUSE VERSUS SIBLING RIVALRY

One of the most common forms of household violence, and one of the least reported, is sibling abuse. Sibling abuse is different from sibling rivalry. In sibling rivalry, both children have an equal opportunity for advantage or disadvantage. Sibling rivalry encourages healthy communication, negotiation, and competition among brothers and sisters.

By comparison, sibling abuse is ongoing, damaging, and tormenting behavior by one sibling with the intent to harm, embarrass, scare, shame, or instill hopelessness in another sibling. It is purposeful, consistent, and severe behavior. In sibling abuse, one sibling always targets the same sibling, there is an intent to harm a sibling physically or emotionally, the abusive sibling is trying to exert control or power over a sibling, and often there is little to no remorse for the behavior.

Sibling abuse can include the following:

- Physical abuse, where one sibling purposefully injures a brother or sister in ways that result in bruises, welts, abrasions, lacerations, wounds, cuts, bone fractures, broken bones, and other examples of physical injury
- Psychological abuse, where one sibling works to demean, belittle, and otherwise challenge the other sibling's self-esteem and self-worth
- Sexual abuse, where one sibling forces sexual acts on or molests another sibling

It is the least reported type of household violence because there are no national laws addressing sibling abuse

(continued on the next page)

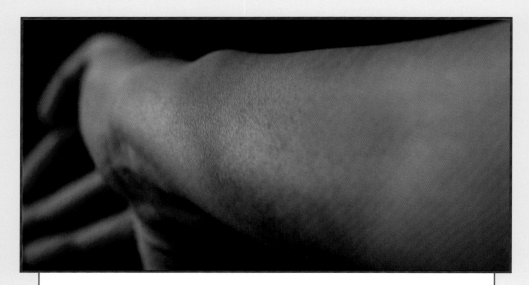

Sibling abuse can sometimes be mistaken for rough play. But repeated bruises and injuries inflicted by one sibling on another is a sign that abuse may be taking place.

(continued from the previous page)

and no nationally accepted or defined definition of sibling abuse. Reports indicating how widespread sibling abuse is are unavailable because there are no national statistics tracking instances that are reported.

Cycle of Violence

The cycle of violence is a commonly recognized pattern of behavior that defines how many abusers act when they are in violent relationships. This pattern of behavior, which often includes phases of tension building and making up and then a period of calm, is often meant to control and intimidate their victims.

Tension building: As an abuser becomes more aggravated, his or her behaviors begin to create tension in a household. The abuser begins to get angry; he or she can become extremely critical of the partner's or their children's behaviors, decisions, or choices; and he or she may become moody or demanding. There is often a breakdown in communication between the abuser and his or her victims where no matter what a victim says to try to explain a situation or calm the abuser, the abuser remains angry. The abuser's behavior often begins to escalate with direct or implied threats of abuse or violence. Victims often feel like nothing they say or do will be right or will help calm

Abuse often follows a cycle where a period of calm and making up occurs after abuse has taken place. This pattern can cause psychological harm to a victim.

the situation. The tension finally becomes too much, and the abuser becomes violent toward his or her victims.

Making up: After an abuser carries out the abuse, he or she may feel some remorse over the violent behavior, apologize for the abuse, and/or promise to never do it again. Abusers may blame the victim for causing the abuse. Sometimes an abuser will deny the abuse took place or will say it was not as bad as the victim claims it was.

Calm: Violence in a household is often irregular, and long periods of calm may go by before another violent incident happens at the hands of an abuser. During this stretch of calm, there is often no abuse or very minor forms of abuse occurring. Many times an abuser will act as if the abuse never happened. Abusers will often make promises to their victims or give them gifts. Victims often are lulled into a false sense of peace, and they begin to hope the abuse has come to an end.

This cycle of abuse can happen hundreds of times in a violent household. Each part of the cycle can vary in length and severity. Sometimes an abuser may stay in one portion of the cycle for hours, days, months, or even years. Often, as time goes on, the making-up and calm stages disappear entirely, and victims live in a constant state of abuse.

CHAPTER 3

The Effects of Living with Household Violence

Lisette Johnson stayed with her abusive husband for more than twenty years while she endured verbal and psychological abuse. Johnson and five other domestic abuse survivors were the subjects of an investigative report by the *Huffington Post*'s Melissa Jelysen on domestic violence and why some women stay with their abusers. For Johnson, her choice to stay centered on one thing: her children.

Johnson's husband told her if she ever tried to leave he'd take the children away from her. Scared of what would happen if her young children were left alone with him, Johnson made the decision to stay so she could protect her young son and daughter.

Over the years, Johnson endured a range of verbal and psychological abuse. Her husband would tell her she was ugly and that she was a bad mother. The children learned to be careful around their father. They learned how to keep him from getting angry. But when her son began repeating abusive language he heard his father say, Johnson decided she had enough. When she finally decided

Children are impressionable victims of household violence. Children who witness abuse, or are victims of abuse, have an increased chance of becoming abusive as adults.

to leave, her husband got a gun, and with her children watching, he shot Johnson twice in the chest and back before killing himself. With her abuser dead, Johnson is now safe, and his torment of her has ended. But the effects of his abuse on their family are ongoing.

Johnson's children have lasting issues from both witnessing years of abuse and from watching their father shoot their mother and kill himself. Her daughter, who was twelve years old at the time of the shooting, deals with depression and suicidal thoughts. Her son, who was nine years old when the shooting occurred, has recurring nightmares and suffers from anxiety and panic attacks. Both are in therapy, and her daughter is taking medication.

Everyone Suffers

In a violent household, the entire family feels the effects of the abuse. Although Johnson's children were not verbally or psychologically abused by their father, the effects of witnessing abuse and watching their mother be belittled and demeaned have been powerful. The effects will last a lifetime as they struggle to make sense of their father's actions and change their own mindsets about what forms a healthy relationship.

Like Johnson's husband, many abusers use threats, intimidation, isolation, and other behaviors to gain and maintain power over their victims. For children, living in an environment of fear, anger, cruelty, or violence can have substantially harmful effects.

Children who live in violent households can have learning issues, exhibit high anxiety, experience feelings of depression and anger, or feel unstable or unsafe in their homes.

OTHER EFFECTS OF VIOLENCE ON CHILDREN

Some children who are exposed to household violence may display failure-to-thrive symptoms. Failure to thrive refers to an infant or young child's inability to meet normal health and developmental milestones, such as weight and growth targets, sitting up, walking, or talking by the appropriate ages. Some children could also:

- Become aggressive or violent toward siblings in ways similar to the abusive parent
- Suffer from low self-esteem
- Have poor impulse control
- Experience academic and learning problems
- Have a disrupted home life if they are forced to flee the house
- Have a fear and distrust of other adults and fail to develop close relationships with others
- Repeat the abuse to others (their partners, spouses, children) when they are older
- Fail to recognize socially acceptable or correct behavior
- Experience psychosomatic complaints, such as stomach pains, headaches, stuttering, and anxiety
- Wet the bed or have other physiological problems

Children who experience household violence can develop severe behavioral problems, become violent as adolescents, continue the cycle of violence in their own relationships, and face mental health issues, such as anxiety, depression, panic attacks, suicidal thoughts, low self-esteem, and poor self-worth.

Children who witness violence in their homes or are victims of household violence may also display the effects of their environment in other emotional, behavioral, social, and physical ways. Emotional responses to violence may include shame and guilt, confusion over their conflicting feelings of love for and fear of a parent, fear of abandonment, feelings of helplessness, and embarrassment. Behaviorally, some children may develop overly aggressive or passive behaviors, act as a parental substitute to the victim parent or to other children in the home, lie, engage in excessive attention-seeking behaviors, manipulate, become overly dependent, and experience mood swings. Socially, children could have difficulty trusting people, develop poor problem-solving skills, become excessive about school or social involvement to avoid their home life, display passivity to bullying or become a bully at school, or engage in exploitive or manipulative relationships. Some children may develop physiological issues, such as nervousness; anxiety; a short attention span; poor personal hygiene, such as infrequent bathing or brushing their teeth; committing self-abuse, such as cutting; or regressing in normal physical development.

Children who witness household violence may also exhibit some extreme or severe behaviors, such as attempting suicide or blaming themselves for the violence, their inability to stop it, and/or their inability to help protect the victim, like their mother or siblings. They are also more likely to abuse alcohol and drugs and to commit sexual assaults and other crimes as teens and adults.

Additional Influences

While the effects of household violence are negative and paint a difficult situation for children living in violent households, not all children exposed to abuse will experience these consequences. Some children are highly resilient. Those who are highly intelligent, have high self-esteem, have a strong and positive relationship with a sibling or another adult, are outgoing, and have a strong sense of social competence are less likely to suffer from the adverse effects of household violence. Other factors that can influence the effect of violence on children include the following:

Children living in violent households are often scared and unsure of their home environment. They can also become withdrawn and develop severe emotional issues.

• **The nature of the violence witnessed by children.** In homes where children witness regular and severe types of violence, children experience higher levels of distress than those who observe less physical abuse and some degree of positive interaction among their parents or guardians.

• **Age of children in the home.** Age has a strong influence on how well children deal with what they witness in a violent home. Younger children often experience higher levels of emotional and psychological distress than older children. Older children may be better able to process the violence they see and may have coping strategies to help them understand what is happening in their home. Younger children are not yet able to understand what is happening.

• **Time since exposure to violence began.** Immediately after a violent encounter, children have higher levels of stress, distress, anxiety, and fear. After some time has passed, those levels drop and the effects of the violence are less noticeable.

• **Gender.** There are key differences in how boys and girls react to household violence. Boys will often externalize, or express their feelings outwardly, through aggressive behaviors, such as acting out, misbehaving, or mimicking household violence at school or on a playground. Girls are more likely to internalize, or keep their feelings hidden or to themselves, and exhibit behaviors such as withdrawal and self-isolation or experience feelings of depression.

• **Being abused versus witnessing abuse.** Children who live in violent households that witness domestic violence and are also abused experience a higher risk for emotional and psychological problems than children who witness violence but are not victims of abuse.

CHAPTER 4

Legal Protections and Rights

You have the right to feel safe in your home. When you're living in a violent household or are the victim of domestic abuse, there are legal rights and protections available. Protective orders can help create a safe space between you and your abuser and give you time to make decisions about how you or your family want to further handle the situation. There are also professionals, such as legal service providers and victim's advocates, who help navigate the complex legal system and offer advice and guidance on how to manage or leave a violent household, outline your legal rights and protections, and help you learn what resources are available to you and your family.

Protective Orders

A protective order (sometimes called a restraining order, protection-from-abuse order, or peace order) can be a helpful tool to victims. A protective order restricts your abuser's access to you. It dictates to your abuser that he or she cannot come within a certain distance of you or your family; it can limit or prevent your abuser's ability to communicate with you or your family via phone, text, mail, or in person; and it can discourage your abuser from stalking or harassing you in any way. Individuals who violate a protective order can face arrest and be punished with fines or jail time.

Getting a protective order differs from state to state. You'll want to research how to apply for a protective order in your state of residence. In general, most states require you to do the following:

- Visit your local law enforcement agency and request a protective order. Usually this involves filing out paperwork and submitting it to the town court or family court office.
- A temporary restraining or protective order may be issued immediately while the court reviews your request for an order.
- A hearing date will be set by the court. At this hearing a judge will listen to you explain why you are requesting a protective or restraining order. This is the time to present any evidence you have collected to support your case. This evidence can include photos of physical abuse, medical records of treatment for physical or sexual abuse, and documentation of incidents where abuse has occurred. Your abuser will be notified of the court date, but he or she is not required to be present.
- A judge will make a decision. If you are granted a permanent restraining or protective order, a copy of the order will usually be given to you before you leave court. A permanent order can restrict your abuser's actions for a set period of time. Some orders can last for several months or several years.
- If your abuser is not present in court, then a copy of the order must be given to him or her, and proof that he or she received the order is necessary.
- Once you have the order, you should provide a copy to your local police department or other law enforcement agencies, as well as your school, college, or place of work. Any location that is

When deciding to leave a violent household, have a plan. Domestic violence hotlines or shelters can help you find a safe place to go and assist in legal matters.

covered by the order should be made aware that you have been issued a restraining order against your abuser.

If you decide to file a protective order and you or your family are still living in the same house as your abuser, you and your family should be prepared to leave your home for a safe place to stay. Even though a protective order is issued to keep an abuser away from you and your family, it is not necessarily an order for the abuser to vacate the family. Your abuser may refuse to leave your home, which means you and your family will need a safe place to go.

Who Can Help You

Making the decision to get help can be a difficult one. There are legal professionals available to help you understand what your rights and legal options are should you decide to leave your home, obtain a protective order, file divorce papers, or file custody orders if you have children. These professionals are highly trained legal representatives who can provide you with the information and guidance you need to make an informed decision.

Legal service providers: Legal service providers are trained professionals who are experts in family law. They are knowledgeable

Legal service providers and victim's advocates can provide you and your family valuable information about your legal rights and where to turn to for a wide variety of services.

about laws, protections, and options you have, and the resources available to you, such as emergency shelters. They can also help you create a safety plan tailored to your situation. They are connected to your local civil or criminal justice system and can help you understand the system and how it works.

Victim's advocate: A victim's advocate supports victims of crimes. These professionals are trained to provide information on your legal rights and protections, offer emotional support, and help victims find the resources they need. They can also work with creditors, landlords, and employers on behalf of victims, can assist in helping victims find shelter and transportation, and even go to court with victims. Victim's advocates also provide documentation and comments to the courts or, if an abuser is serving jail time, to a parole board. They also can assist in explaining and helping you complete legal paperwork, contact support organizations on your behalf, and arrange for social services to provide assistance to you and your family.

You can find victim's advocates in a variety of places. Some are employed by the justice system and work at police stations, in prosecutor's offices, for the courts, for probation or parole departments, or in prisons. They can also be found at nonprofit organizations that provide services to victims, such as sexual assault crisis centers, domestic violence programs, or women's centers. Advocates can be paid or volunteer, but most have earned an academic degree in an area such as social work, psychology, women's studies, criminal justice, education, or law.

Law enforcement: Your local police department can intervene in domestic violence situations. If you call 911 to report a domestic disturbance, when officers arrive they can help mediate an argument, arrest an individual if a law has been broken, or take an abuser into custody if the victim decides to press charges. If a

If law enforcement responds to a domestic violence incident, they can arrest or take the abuser into custody and file a report. Their report helps if the victim presses charges.

serious enough assault has taken place, the victim may not have a choice in pressing charges. Officers have the ability to arrest an individual if they feel he or she poses a threat or has committed a crime. In the short term, an abuser may be arrested and held in jail until he or she can post bail, which could be as little as a few hours or as long as a few days. But it is important to take legal action and press charges immediately—otherwise your decision to let an incident go may make it more difficult for law enforcement to protect you. Law enforcement can provide the following protections and services to you and your family:

- Help you and your family members leave your home safely.
- Arrest your abuser if they have enough evidence that he or she has committed a crime against you.
- Arrest your abuser if a protection or restraining order has been violated.
- Provide you with information on domestic violence programs and emergency shelters.

IF YOU CALL 911 TO REPORT ABUSE

If you decide to call law enforcement officials to report household violence, you should know they can help protect you. But be prepared to help them understand your case. When the police come, tell them everything the abuser did that made you call.

- If you have been hit, tell the police where and if a weapon was used. Tell them how many times it happened. Show them any physical marks or injuries on your body. Some physical injuries, such as bruises, can take some time to show up on your body. Marks may take time to show up. If you see a mark after the police leave, call them and request that they take pictures of the bruises. This photo evidence may be used in court.
- If your abuser has broken or destroyed any property, show the police and take photographs of the damaged goods.
- When police respond to a call, they must compete a

report that outlines what happened to you. Police reports can be used in court if your abuser is charged with a crime. You also have access to these reports and should obtain one for each time you have had to call law enforcement. Keep them in a safe place in case you ever need to use them in court or offer evidence of previously reported domestic disturbances.

- All officers carry identification. Note the officers' names and badge numbers.
- All police reports are numbered. Get the report number before the officers leave your home so you can request a copy of it once it's been filed.

Stand-Your-Ground Laws

More than twenty states have passed "stand-your-ground" laws. These laws authorize individuals to use deadly force if they find themselves in a life-threatening situation in which they must use self-defense. Some prosecutors are arguing that stand-your-ground laws should not apply in domestic violence incidents that happen in the home and could lead to unreasonable use of the law.

A case of domestic abuse drew attention to the stand-your ground-law in South Carolina when Whitlee Jones stabbed and killed Eric Lee, her boyfriend, in self-defense. One evening, Jones was screaming as Lee dragged her down the street by her hair. Jones's calls for help prompted a neighbor to call the police. When the officer arrived, the argument had already ended, and Jones had fled the scene to get away from her boyfriend. Jones returned to her home later in the evening with the intent of packing her belongings and leaving her boyfriend. In addition to clothing and personal items, Jones packed a knife to protect herself. As she left the house, Lee attacked her, and Jones stabbed him once in self-defense. Lee died.

A judge sided with Jones and her attorney, who claimed Jones's use of deadly force was within the definition of the stand-your-ground law. The judge exempted Jones from a trial, and she was not charged in Lee's murder. However, a prosecutor is appealing the judge's decision. Several other cases of domestic violence, including one that involved one roommate killing another, are drawing attention to the law and the possibility that it either needs to be better defined or it should include provisions for violent acts committed within a home that involve spouses, family members, roommates, or those in some sort of defined relationship, such as couples who live together.

CHAPTER 5

Getting Help

For Gabbe Rowland, the abuse progressed quickly once it started. It began with belittling, name-calling, and manipulation. Soon it escalated to physical violence with Rowland's boyfriend hitting her and pulling her hair. He became controlling, often telling her what she could and could not do.

Rowland's boyfriend had a history of drug abuse. One night he decided he wanted Rowland to take heroin with him. Although she resisted and begged him to stop, Rowland's boyfriend injected her with the drug. For the next five days, Rowland's boyfriend injected her with heroin every day and tortured her. Repeatedly, he beat her, raped her, and threatened to kill her. Rowland eventually found her way to her job, where she told her boss about the abuse. Her boss encouraged her to go to the police station and report the abuse, forced drug use, and assaults. Rowland pressed charges, and her boyfriend is now serving six years in jail.

It's important to remember that you are not to blame for being abused. No matter what your abuser may say, there is never a reason for someone to be violent toward you or your family.

Tell Someone

If you live in a violent household, if you are the victim of abuse, or if one parent is abusive toward another, it's important to seek

If you live in a violent household, talk to a trusted adult or teacher, religious leader, or school counselor. Local or national hotlines are available for advice and help.

help immediately. Talk to a trusted adult, such as a friend's parent, your religious leader, a coach, a teacher, a school nurse, or a guidance counselor. Share with this person what you and your family have been experiencing. If you choose to tell someone about the abuse, be aware that some adults—teachers, counselors, school nurses, doctors, and other medical staff—are mandatory reporters of abuse. This means that these professionals are legally required to report any and all instances of domestic violence, child abuse, dating abuse, and sexual abuse to local law enforcement or a child

10 GREAT QUESTIONS TO ASK
WHEN YOU'RE ASKING FOR HELP

1. If I ask for help, will the parent who is abusive find out?

2. How do I get out of my house safety?

3. How do I help my family get out of a violent household?

4. Where can my family and I go to feel safe?

5. What will happen if I report the abuse to law enforcement?

6. How can I be in love with someone who hurts me?

7. How can parents abuse their children?

8. What if no one believes me about the abuse or if my abused parent denies the abuse is happening?

9. My friend is being abused at home. How can I help?

10. Can abusers get help and change?

protective services agency. Those who are mandatory reporters are not allowed, by law, to keep your secret, even if they want to. Don't let this discourage you from talking to someone about the abuse you are experiencing. Teachers, counselors, local law enforcement officials, and others can help you find the resources you need to talk through and understand what is happening, help you create a plan of safety or a plan of escape, and provide you and your family with support.

HOW HOTLINES CAN HELP

According to the National Coalition Against Domestic Violence, crisis hotlines provide a range of services that include the following:

Crisis Intervention Services

- Highly trained professionals are available to provide information and access to area resources designed to assist victims of domestic abuse.
- Access to emergency shelters and other residential facilities should you or your family members require a safe place to stay.
- Medical services to ensure any injuries sustained from physical abuse are treated and documented.
- Access to emergency shelters or other secure residential facilities.
- Transportation networks to help you or your family safely get to and from appointments.
- Legal advice on laws relating to domestic violence and help filling out paperwork and filing legal documents.

- Assistance in removing perpetrators from the home or in arranging safe passage for you and your family to a secure location.

Emotional Support Services
- Support groups for self-help.
- Counseling for you, your parents, and your siblings or other children living in the home.
- Training in assertiveness for victims to feel more in control of their surroundings and to become more proactive in defending themselves.
- Self-esteem and confidence-building classes to help you gain your life back.

Advocacy and Legal Assistance
- Access to your children.
- Assistance in arranging custody and visitation for children.
- Advice on property and ownership of home.
- Financial support and guidance.
- Help seeking restraining or protective orders and completing the required paperwork.
- Assistance in obtaining public assistance or unemployment benefits.

Other Services
- Access to housing and safe lodgings.
- Assistance arranging care for children.
- Information on and access to community services and resources.

Deciding to Seek Help

When you decide you are ready to seek help, there are many different agencies and organizations available to help. If you need help deciding whom you should talk to, your first step is to call a local or national domestic violence crisis hotline.

Crisis hotlines are open twenty-four hours a day, seven days a week. They are also free to call. Hotlines are staffed with highly trained professionals to whom you can talk confidentially about

A crisis hotline can provide advice and support, connect you to local resources, and help you and your family devise a plan to leave a violent household.

the abuse you are experiencing. They will share information and resources with you, help you create a plan of safety to help keep you safe while you are living in your home, and provide you with advice and guidance on how to leave a violent household.

If You and Your Family Plan to Leave

Deciding to leave a violent household can be a serious and difficult decision for you and your family. It's not a decision to be made lightly or without some sort of plan in place. The most threatening time for someone who is being abused is when he or she leaves. Your abuser is not only angry but has lost control over his or her victims. This is often when the most severe abuse and violence can happen.

You need a safe place to go, and you must be prepared in order to keep yourself and your family safe.

Somewhere safe: Is there a safe place to stay where your abuser will not be able to find you? This could be a women's shelter, an apartment in a nearby town or city, or a family member or friend's house.

What to take along: If you and your family leave a violent household, take important papers and documents with you, such as social

If your family decides to leave, your mother or father should gather important documents, such as birth certificates, health insurance information, financial statements, and any evidence of abuse.

security cards, birth certificates, marriage license, leases or deeds to property, financial and bank statements, insurance policies, and pay stubs to prove income. Also take any past evidence of abuse, such as photos, police reports, or medical records. You will need these items if you or one of your parents plans to file legal paperwork or apply for public assistance.

How to be safe again: If you and your family stay in your home and the abuser is forced to leave, you should change the locks, screen all phone calls, document all contact or incidences involving your abuser, create a plan for getting away should you be confronted by your abuser, notify work and school of the situation, and vary your routine. You may also want to keep a cell phone on you at all times, make sure you have important numbers memorized, and have a mental list of safe people to contact in an emergency.

Helping a Friend

If you know someone who is living in a violent household or is being abused in some way, you can help:

- Acknowledge the situation and be supportive.
- Don't be judgmental. Never ask why he or she doesn't just leave.
- Ask how you can help.
- Encourage your friend to seek help. Offer to be with your friend when he or she calls a crisis hotline.
- Educate yourself about household violence.
- Avoid any confrontations with your friend's abuser. This interaction could be dangerous for you and your friend.
- Help your friend create a safety plan.
- Remember that no matter how much you want to see your friend and his or her family to be safe, you cannot rescue them.

It's natural to want to help a friend in need. Be supportive and encourage your friend to seek guidance from a trusted adult, but steer clear of your friend's abuser.

A Safe and Happy Future

No one expects to live with an abusive parent or partner. If you find yourself in an abusive relationship or in an unsafe living situation, there are resources available to you and your family to get you the help you need to break free of the abuse and begin to rebuild your life. Household violence can shape your life, and its effects can last a lifetime. Learn how you can avoid violent situations at home, find out what your rights are, and educate yourself on the signs of violent and controlling behavior. Know where you can go to be safe and the people you can count on for support if you decide to leave a violent household. These steps will help you move forward toward the safe and happy future you deserve.

ADVOCATE A person who argues on behalf of another person in a court of law.

ALLEGED Charged with, but not proven guilty of, having done something illegal or wrong.

CONSEQUENCE Something that occurs because of an action or decision.

COPING STRATEGIES Specific behavioral and psychological efforts that people use to deal with, endure, or lessen stressful events.

CUSTODY The legal claim to care for a child as well as make all decisions on behalf of the child.

DEMEAN To make someone feel lower in personality, rank, or standing.

EXTERNALIZE To come up with an explanation for, or rationalize, something by relating it to causes outside oneself.

HUMILIATION Making someone feel lower in one's or another person's view.

IMPRESSIONABLE Influenced or affected with ease.

INTERNALIZE To keep a problem inside and, as a result, change your behaviors based on your assessment of your feelings about the problem.

LACERATION A deep wound of the skin.

MISDEMEANOR A crime that is not as serious as a felony.

PASSIVE Not responding to or resisting, as well as tolerating or allowing the actions of others or what happens.

PHYSIOLOGICAL Characteristic of healthy or normal functioning of the body.

PROSECUTOR A lawyer who represents the victim in a court case, or a lawyer who tries to prove the defendant is guilty of a crime.

PSYCHOSOMATIC Relating to or involving physical symptoms resulting from a mental or emotional disruption.

REGRESS To go back, usually to a previous state or stage.

RESILIENT Having the ability to return to being strong and healthy after a negative experience.

SOCIAL COMPETENCE Mature social, intellectual, and behavioral skill sets.

STUTTERING A speech problem that causes uncontrollable repetition of the beginning sound of certain words.

VOLATILE Extreme, unexpected, or sudden changes of behavior caused by uncontrolled emotions, or quickly becoming dangerously out of control.

Break the Cycle
P.O. Box 66165
Washington, DC 20035
(202) 824-0707
Website: http://www.breakthecycle.org
Break the Cycle is the foremost national nonprofit organization
that provides information about domestic violence and
dating violence to teens and young adults.

Canadian Women's Foundation, Toronto Office
133 Richmond Street W, Suite 504
Toronto, ON M5H 2L3
Canada
(866) 293-4483
Website: http://www.canadianwomen.org
The Canadian Women's Foundation works to strengthen and
empower the women and girls who are in the most need,
such as those in violent situations.

National Center on Domestic and Sexual Violence (NCDSV)
4612 Shoal Creek Boulevard
Austin, TX 78756
(800) 799-SAFE (7233)
Website: http://www.ncdsv.org
The NCDSV's mission is to guide national policy to protect victims
of domestic violence and to offer training and discussion to the
wide variety of professionals working with and for victims of
domestic violence.

National Coalition Against Domestic Violence (NCADV)
One Broadway, Suite B210
Denver, CO 80203
(303) 839-1852
Website: http://www.ncadv.org
The NCADV strives to build local, regional, and national support
    services for domestic violence victims and to increase the
    education and awareness of domestic violence and its effects
    on a community. It also assists in developing policies and
    collaborates on legislative actions aimed at protecting women
    and families.

The National Domestic Violence Hotline
P.O. Box 161810
Austin, TX 78716
(800) 799-SAFE (7233)
Website: http://www.thehotline.org
Open seven days a week, the National Domestic Violence
    Hotline is confidential and free for victims to use to find
    support, guidance, resources, and emergency services.

National Online Resource Center for Violence
    Against Women (VAWnet)
3605 Vartan Way, Suite 101
Harrisburg, PA 17110
(800) 537-2238
Website: http://www.vawnet.org
VAWnet is a complete collection of online materials and
    information on domestic violence, sexual violence, and
    similar matters.

Violence Against Women, Services Elgin County
300 Talbot Street, Suite 26
St. Thomas, ON N5P 4E2
Canada
(800) 265-4305
Website: http://www.vawsec.on.ca
Open twenty-four hours a day, this organization supports
    women and children, offering free and confidential help,
    shelter, and counseling, with a goal of working to provide a
    safer community for everyone.

Websites

Because of the changing nature of Internet links, Rosen Publishing has developed an online list of websites related to the subject of this book. This site is updated regularly. Please use this link to access the list:

http://www.rosenlinks.com/CVAW/House

FOR FURTHER READING

Abrahams, Hilary. *Rebuilding Lives After Domestic Violence: Understanding Long-Term Outcomes*. London, England: Jessica Kingsley Publishers, 2010.

Abrahams, Hilary. *Supporting Women After Domestic Violence: Loss, Trauma and Recovery*. London, England: Jessica Kingsley Publishers, 2007.

Coleman Carter, Toni L. *When Trouble Finds You: Overcoming Child Abuse, Teen Pregnancy, Domestic Violence, and Discovering the Remarkable Power of the Human Spirit*. Highland Park, IL: RTC Publishing, 2013.

Creighton, Allan, and Paul Kivel. *Helping Teens Stop Violence, Build Community, and Stand for Justice*. Nashville, TN: Hunter House Publishing, 2011.

Hines, Denise A., Kathleen Malley-Morrison, and Leila B. Dutton. *Family Violence in the United States: Defining, Understanding, and Combating Abuse*. Thousand Oaks, CA: Sage Publishing, 2012.

Hunter, Joanna V. *But He'll Change: End the Thinking That Keeps You in an Abusive Relationship*. Center City, MN: Hazelden Publishing, 2010.

Klein, Rebecca. *Rape and Sexual Assault: Healing and Recovery*. New York, NY: Rosen Publishing Group, 2013.

Lawton, Sandra Augustyn. *Abuse and Violence Information for Teens: Health Tips About the Causes and Consequences of Abusive and Violent Behavior*. Detroit, MI: Omnigraphics, Inc., 2007.

Lily, Henrietta M. *Teen Mental Health: Dating Violence*. New York, NY: Rosen Publishing Group, 2011.

Mabry Gordon, Sherri. *Beyond Bruises: The Truth About Teens and Abuse*. Berkeley Heights, NJ: Enslow Publishers, 2009.

Michaels, Vanessa Lynn, and Jeremy Harrow. *Frequently Asked Questions About Family Violence*. New York, NY: Rosen Publishing Group, 2011.

Murray, Jill A. *But He Never Hit Me: The Devastating Cost of Non-Physical Abuse to Girls and Women*. Bloomington, IN: iUniverse, 2007.

BIBLIOGRAPHY

Alabama Coalition Against Domestic Violence. "The Effects of DV on Children." Retrieved November 9, 2014 (http://www.acadv.org/children.html).

Boren, Cindy. "Hope Solo Arrest: Nephew Says She Was Drinking, Called Him 'Too Fat to Be an Athlete.'" *Washington Post*, June 24, 2014. Retrieved November 17, 2014 (http://www.washingtonpost.com/blogs/early-lead/wp/2014/06/24/hope-solo-arrest-nephew-says-she-was-drinking-called-him-fat-and-unathletic).

Child Welfare Information Gateway. "Impact of Domestic Violence on Children." Children's Bureau, Administration for Children and Families, U.S. Department of Health and Human Services, 2009. Retrieved November 14, 2014 (https://www.childwelfare.gov/pubs/factsheets/domestic_violence/impact.cfm).

DomesticViolence.org. "What Can I Do to Be Safe?" 2009. Retrieved November 9, 2014 (http://www.domesticviolence.org/what-can-i-do-to-be-safe).

Flatlow, Nicole. "South Carolina Prosecutors Say Stand Your Ground Doesn't Apply to Victims of Domestic Violence." ThinkProgress, October 15, 2014. Retrieved November 12, 2014 (http://thinkprogress.org/justice/2014/10/14/3579407/south-carolina-prosecutors-say-stand-your-ground-doesnt-apply-to-victims-of-domestic-violence).

Georgia Coalition Against Domestic Violence. "Domestic Violence Myths and Facts." Retrieved November 5, 2014 (http://gcadv.org/general-resources/common-myths-about-domestic-violence).

"Getting Help." National Coalition Against Domestic Violence, 2011. Retrieved November 12, 2014 (http://www.ncadv.org/protectyourself/GettingHelp.php).

Grey, Jeff. "Adrian Peterson Indicted for Reckless or Negligent Injury to Child, per Report." SB Nation, September 12, 2014. Retrieved November 14, 2014 (http://www.sbnation.com/nfl/2014/9/12/6141819/adrian-peterson-arrest-child-injury-houston/in/5906378).

Jelysen, Melissa. "'Why Didn't You Just Leave?': Six Domestic Violence Survivors Explain Why It's Never That Simple." *Huffington Post*, September 12, 2014. Retrieved November 14, 2014 (http://www.huffingtonpost.com/2014/09/12/why-didnt-you-just-leave_n_5805134.html).

Mayo Clinic Staff. "Domestic Violence Against Women: Recognize Patterns, Seek Help." Mayo Clinic, 2014. Retrieved November 18, 2014 (http://www.mayoclinic.org/healthy-living/adult-health/in-depth/domestic-violence/art-20048397).

National Center for Victims of Crime. "What Is a Victim Advocate?" 2012. Retrieved November 7, 2014 (http://www.victimsofcrime.org/help-for-crime-victims/get-help-bulle-tins-for-crime-victims/what-is-a-victim-advocate-).

National Coalition Against Domestic Violence. "Safety Plan." 2011. Retrieved November 5, 2014 (http://www.ncadv.org/protectyourself/SafetyPlan.php).

NFL.com. "Adrian Peterson's Appeal Set for Monday." November 13, 2014. Retrieved November 14, 2014 (http://www.nfl.com/news/story/0ap3000000427324/article/adrian-petersons-appeals-hearing-set-for-monday).

Rodriguez, Jayson. "Rihanna Details Chris Brown Assault in '20/20' Interview." MTV, November 7, 2009. Retrieved November 14, 2014 (http://www.mtv.com/news/1625783/rihanna-details-chris-brown-assault-in-2020-interview).

Safe Horizon. "Domestic Violence Statistics and Facts." 2014.

    Retrieved November 14, 2014 (http://www.safehorizon.org/
    page/domestic-violence-statistics--facts-52.html).

United States Department of Justice. "What Is Domestic
    Violence?" Retrieved November 12, 2014 (http://www
    .justice.gov/ovw/domestic-violence).

World Health Organization. "Violence Prevention, the Evidence:
    Changing Cultural and Social Norms That Support
    Violence." 2009. Retrieved November 9, 2014 (http://www
    .who.int/violence_injury_prevention/violence/norms.pdf).

About the Author

Laura La Bella is a writer and the author of more than twenty-five nonfiction children's books. She has profiled actress and activist Angelina Jolie in *Celebrity Activists: Angelina Jolie Goodwill Ambassador to the UN*; reported on the declining availability of the world's fresh water supply in *Not Enough to Drink: Pollution, Drought, and Tainted Water Supplies*; and examined the food industry in *Safety and the Food Supply*. La Bella lives in Rochester, New York, with her husband and two sons.

Photo Credits

Cover © Tetra Images/Getty Images; p. 5 Gregg DeGuire/WireImage/Getty Images; p. 7 Suzi Pratt/Getty Images; p. 9 schafar/iStock/Thinkstock; p. 11 lofilolo/iStock/Thinkstock; p. 14 Tadamasa Taniguchi/The Image Bank/Getty Images; p. 20 Photographee.eu/Shutterstock.com; p. 22 Frank Gaertner/Shutterstock.com; p. 23 BGF Images/Getty Images; p. 26 Ghislain & Marie David de Lossy/The Image Bank/Getty Images; p. 27 Aaron-H/iStock/iStock/Thinkstock; p. 30 monkeybusinessimages/iStock/Thinkstock; p. 34 Reggie Casagrande/Photographer's Choice RF/Getty Images; p. 35 © iStockphoto.com/4774344sean; p. 37 asiseeit/Vetta/Getty Images; p. 42 Ghislain & Marie David de Lossy/Cultura/Getty Images; p. 46 Yuanting/iStock/Thinkstock; p. 47 © iStockphoto.com/KM6064; p. 49 Feverpitched/iStock/Thinkstock

Designer: Nicole Russo; Editor: Heather Moore Niver